Nigeria

ALISON BROWNLIE

RSVP

RAINTREE
STECK-VAUGHN
P U B L I S H E R S
A Steck-Vaughn Company

Austin, Texas

www.steck-vaughn.com

WE COME FROM

Brazil • China • France
Germany • India • Jamaica • Japan
Kenya • Nigeria • South Africa

The family you are about to meet lives in a city called Lagos. Like any other country, Nigeria has many different lifestyles. People live in the countryside as well as in towns and cities.

Cover: Morning assembly in an elementary school near Lagos
Title page (top to bottom): A busy street in Lagos; a farm in the countryside; the central mosque in Abuja; a man climbing a tree to pick coconuts; a girl selling bread in the market in Lagos
Contents page: Two Nigerian boys
Index: Nnedima and her cousins in their best clothes, ready to go to church

Published by Raintree Steck-Vaughn Publishers, an imprint of Steck-Vaughn Company

Picture Acknowledgments: Associated Press/Topham 9; Axiom *contents page*, 20 (bottom)/James Morris, 22/James Morris, 29 (top right)/Guy Marks; Hutchison 19 (bottom)/ Juliet Highet, 20 (top)/Anna Tully; Panos *cover*, 21/Betty Press; Still Pictures 23/Mark Edwards; Wayland Picture Library 6, 7(top), 8 (bottom)/James Morris, 26 (top); Morounke Williams *title page* (second from bottom), 8 (top). All the other photographs are by Pierre Chuckwudi Alozie.
The map on page 5 is by Peter Bull.

Library of Congress Cataloging-in-Publication Data

Brownlie, Alison.
Nigeria / Alison Brownlie.
    p.   cm.—(We come from)
    Includes bibliographical references and index.
    ISBN 0-8172-5513-3
    1. Nigeria—Juvenile literature.
    [1. Nigeria.]
    I. Title. II. Series.
    DT515.22.B76 2000
    966.9—dc21   99-23157

Printed in Italy. Bound in the United States.
1 2 3 4 5 6 7 8 9 0 04 03 02 01 00

Contents

Welcome to Nigeria!

> "My name is Nnedima. In this photo, I'm wearing my best pink dress for church."

Nnedima ▶ (pronounced "Ned-im-a") with her aunt and four of her cousins

Nnedima is eleven years old. She lives in Ikeja, a suburb of the city of Lagos. You can see where Lagos is on the map on page 5. Nnedima's parents live far away in Umuahia, a village in eastern Nigeria. Nnedima lives with her aunt, uncle, and cousins.

▼ *Nigeria is a very big country. One-fourth of all Africans live here.*

▲ *Nigeria's place in the world*

NIGERIA

Capital city	Abuja
Land area	356,667 sq. mi. (923,768 sq. km)
Population	104 million people (1996 estimate)
Main languages	English (official), Hausa, Ibo, and Yoruba
Main religions	Islam in the north, Christianity in the south

5

Land and Weather

Most of Nigeria is flat. There are some low mountains in the east and around the center of the country.

A hot, dry wind from the Sahara blows across northern Nigeria. There is little rain, so only a few trees grow on the grassy plains.

▼ *The Jos Plateau in central Nigeria*

▲ *The Seven Stream waterfall in southern Nigeria*

As you travel south, the land becomes greener. At certain times of the year, there is a lot of rain here, so more trees and plants are able to grow.

▶ *The roads are sometimes damaged by floods in the rainy season.*

Thick rain forest grows in southern Nigeria. Along the coast there are sandy beaches and areas of very wet land, called swamps.

Plants called mangroves grow in the swamps. Their tangled roots grow high above the ground.

▲ *The coast is lined with palm trees.*

▼ *Heavy rain helps the rain forest grow.*

"Lagos is the biggest city in Nigeria."—Nnedima

Many of the towns and cities are in the south. Lagos, where Nnedima lives, is a busy port. Most of the city is built on an island.

At Home

Most Nigerians live in the countryside, in houses made of blocks of earth. A child's parents, grandparents, aunts, and uncles usually live together in a compound. A compound is a group of small houses, built around a central yard.

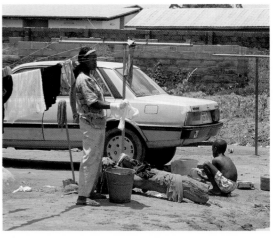

▲ *A woman washes clothes and hangs them out to dry.*

▼ *Houses made of earth stay cool in the heat of the day.*

▶ *One-fourth of all Nigerians live in the towns and cities.*

▲ *Nnedima's aunt does chores outdoors.*

Nnedima lives in Lagos with her aunt and uncle so that she can go to school. She also helps her aunt look after the younger children.

Nnedima shares a bedroom with one of her cousins. There are two other bedrooms, a living room, a kitchen, and a bathroom in her uncle's apartment.

▶ *Nnedima's aunt and cousins in their living room*

"I like to watch children's programs on TV."—Nnedima

Nigerian Food

Nigerians are able to grow most of the food they need in their own country. Yams are an important food. A yam is a vegetable like a potato and can be boiled, roasted, or pounded.

▶ *These farmers are preparing the ground so that they can plant yams.*

▼ *Piles of yams on sale in the market in Lagos*

14

Nigerians like spicy, peppery food.
They enjoy soups and stews made
with vegetables, beans, and fish.

In the villages, people usually grow their own food. But Nnedima's aunt has to go to the market every day to buy fresh vegetables, meat, and fish. Sometimes Nnedima goes to the market to get bread.

◀ *Nnedima's cousin slices vegetables to make soup.*

"I help my aunt by washing the vegetables for dinner."—Nnedima

At Work

In the countryside, most people are farmers. They grow rice, corn, yams, and cassavas, and they keep chickens and goats. In the north many people herd sheep and goats. They move from place to place, looking for fresh pasture for their animals.

▼ *Farmers go to the market to sell the food that their own families do not need.*

Many young people move to the cities to look for work. They may get jobs in offices, factories, or stores.

▲ *A tailor making clothes in Lagos*

▼ *Women at work in a busy bank in Lagos*

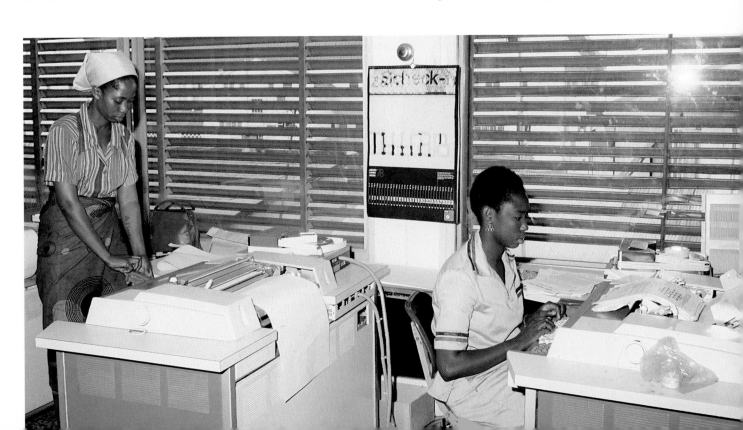

At School

Until a few years ago, children used to learn from the older people in their villages. Now, most children go to school to learn.

▶ *Classes often have more than forty pupils.*

"My favorite subject is English."—Nnedima

The school day starts early, at eight o'clock in the morning. Most children go home for lunch. School usually finishes by two o'clock because it is too hot to work in the afternoon.

▲ Sometimes classes take place outside.

21

All Nnedima's classes are in English, but at home she often speaks Ibo with her relatives. At school she learns about the history and geography of Nigeria as well as doing math, science, and sports.

▶ *Most children walk home from school.*

▼ *Schoolchildren playing outside their school*

UGBOWO PRIMARY SCHOOL

UGBOWO ~ BENIN CITY

23

Free Time

People in Nigeria enjoy many festivals. At celebrations such as weddings and naming ceremonies, there is lots of singing and dancing.

People who live in the towns and cities can go to the movies, or they can visit a museum.

▲ *The whole family enjoys a visit to the museum.*

◀ *These teenagers in Lagos are having a pedalo race.*

24

"I go to church with my aunt and my cousins every Sunday."—Nnedima

25

Looking Ahead

In the last few years, Nigeria has been ruled by a dictator. Many people would like to be able to choose a new leader.

There is lots of oil in Nigeria. In the future Nigerians hope that their country will get more money from selling the oil. Then they might be able to build better roads, schools, and hospitals.

▲ *Many Nigerians work in the oil industry.*

▼ *Abuja has been the capital of Nigeria since 1991.*

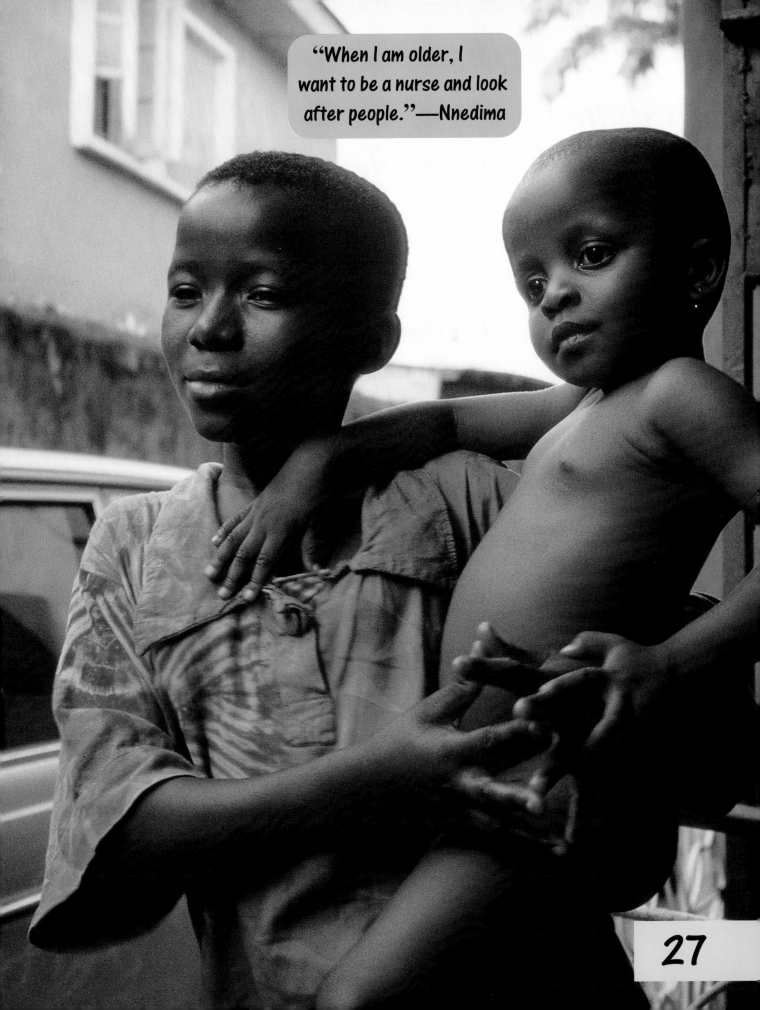

27

Hide-and-seek

Nnedima likes to play hide-and-seek with her cousins and her friends from the apartment upstairs. In Nigeria hide-and-seek is called *b'oju b'oju*.

To play hide-and-seek, close your eyes and count to 100. While you are doing this, all your friends must find somewhere to hide.

▲ *Nnedima with her cousins and friends*

When you have counted to 100, open your eyes and see how quickly you can find your friends.

Nnedima usually finds her friends quickly, but her cousin Ichioma is very good at finding places to hide. It takes Nnedima a long while to find her.

◀ *Nnedima and her friends run off to hide.*

Nigeria Fact File

◀ Money facts
Nigeria's money is the naira. There are 100 kobo in 1 naira. $1 is worth about 33 naira.

▶ Benin bronzes
This is one of the famous Benin bronzes. Most of these beautiful figures were made in Nigeria about 300 years ago.

▼ Population
Nigeria has the largest population in Africa. The population is made up of more than 250 ethnic groups. The largest groups are the Fulani, the Hausa, the Yoruba, and the Ibo. Each group has its own customs; many groups have their own language, too.

Independence Day
Nigeria was ruled by Great Britain for many years, but it became independent on October 1, 1960. October 1 is now a national holiday.

▼ The Nigerian flag
The colors in the Nigerian flag have special meanings. The green represents farming and the richness of the land. The white represents peace.

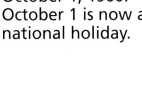

Soccer
Soccer is the most popular sport in Nigeria. The national team, the Super Eagles, made it to the final rounds of the 1998 World Cup.

Glossary

Desert A very dry area of land, where only a few plants and animals can survive.

Dictator Someone who takes command of a country without having been chosen by the people.

Ethnic group A group of people who share the same language and customs.

Mosque A place where Muslims go to pray and hold religious ceremonies.

Naming ceremony A ceremony at which a baby is given its name.

Pedalo A small boat that has pedals to make it move.

Plains Areas of flat land.

Plateau An area of high, fairly flat land.

Rain forest Thick forest that grows in places where the weather is hot and very wet all year round.

Suburb An area of a town or city where people live, away from the center.

Further Information

Books:

Adeeb, Hassan and Adeeb, Bonnetta: *Nigeria: One Nation, Many Cultures* (Exploring Cultures of the World). Tarrytown, NY: Benchmark Books, 1996.

Bailey, Donna. *Nigeria* (Where We Live). Austin, TX: Raintree Steck-Vaughn, 1990

Oluonye, Mary N. *Nigeria* (Ticket to). Minneapolis, MN: Carolrhoda Books, 1998

Owhonda, John. *Nigeria: A Nation of Many Peoples* (Discovering Our Heritage). New York: Dillon Press, 1997.

Tenquist, Alasdair. *Nigeria* (Economically Developing Countries). Austin, TX: Raintree Steck-Vaughn, 1996.

Organizations:

Nigerian Embassy
2201 M Street NW
Washington, DC 20037

Index

All the numbers in **bold** refer to illustrations.